50 Q

Modelling

By Mike Gershon

About the Author

Mike Gershon is an expert educationalist who works throughout the UK and abroad helping teachers to develop their practice. His knowledge of teaching and learning is rooted in the practicalities of the classroom and his online teaching tools have been viewed and downloaded more than 3.5 million times, making them some of the most popular of all time.

He is the author of over 80 books and guides covering different areas of teaching and learning. Some of Mike's bestsellers include books on assessment for learning, questioning, differentiation and outstanding teaching, as well as Growth Mindsets. You can train online with Mike, from anywhere in the world, at www.tes.com/institute/cpd-courses-teachers.

You can also find out more at www.mikegershon.com and www.gershongrowthmindsets.com, including about Mike's inspirational in-school training and student workshops.

Training and Consultancy

Mike offers a range of training and consultancy services covering all areas of teaching and learning, raising achievement and classroom practice. He runs inspiring and engaging INSET in primary schools, secondary schools and colleges. Examples of recent training events include:

- Growth Mindsets: Theory and Practice – William Bellamy Primary School, Dagenham
- Creating a Challenge Culture: Stretch and Challenge Reimagined – Manchester College
- Rethinking Differentiation – The British School of Brussels

To find out more, visit www.mikegershon.com or www.gershongrowthmindsets.com or get in touch via mike@mikegershon.com

Other Works from the Same Author

Available to buy now on Amazon:

How to Develop Growth Mindsets in the Classroom: The Complete Guide

How to use Differentiation in the Classroom: The Complete Guide

How to use Assessment for Learning in the Classroom: The Complete Guide

How to use Bloom's Taxonomy in the Classroom: The Complete Guide

How to use Questioning in the Classroom: The Complete Guide

How to use Discussion in the Classroom: The Complete Guide

How to Manage Behaviour in the Classroom: The Complete Guide

How to Teach EAL Students in the Classroom: The Complete Guide

How to be an Outstanding Trainee Teacher: The Complete Guide

More Secondary Starters and Plenaries

Secondary Starters and Plenaries: History

Teach Now! History: Becoming a Great History Teacher

The Growth Mindset Pocketbook (with Professor Barry Hymer)

The Exams, Tests and Revision Pocketbook

Also available to buy now on Amazon, the entire 'Quick 50' Series:

50 Quick Ways to Get Past 'I Don't Know'

50 Quick Ways to Start Your Lessons with a Bang!

50 Quick Ways to Improve Literacy Across the Curriculum

50 Quick Ways to Improve Feedback and Marking

50 Quick Ways to Use Scaffolding and Modelling

50 Quick Ways to Stretch and Challenge More-Able Students

50 Quick Ways to Create Independent Learners

50 Quick Ways to go from Good to Outstanding

50 Quick Ways to Support Less-Able Learners

50 Quick and Brilliant Teaching Ideas

50 Quick and Brilliant Teaching Techniques

50 Quick and Easy Lesson Activities

50 Quick Ways to Help Your Students Secure A and B Grades at GCSE

50 Quick Ways to Help Your Students Think, Learn, and Use Their Brains Brilliantly

50 Quick Ways to Motivate and Engage Your Students

50 Quick Ways to Outstanding Teaching

50 Quick Ways to Perfect Behaviour Management

50 Quick and Brilliant Teaching Games

50 Quick and Easy Ways Leaders Can Prepare for Ofsted

50 Quick and Easy Ways to Outstanding Group Work

50 Quick and Easy Ways to Prepare for Ofsted

About the Series

The 'Quick 50' series was born out of a desire to provide teachers with practical, tried and tested ideas, activities, strategies and techniques which would help them to teach brilliant lessons, raise achievement and engage and inspire their students.

Every title in the series distils great teaching wisdom into fifty bite-sized chunks. These are easy to digest and easy to apply – perfect for the busy teacher who wants to develop their practice and support their students.

Acknowledgements

My thanks to all the staff and students I have worked with past and present, particularly those at Pimlico Academy and King Edward VI School, Bury St Edmunds. Thanks also to the teachers and teaching assistants who have attended my training sessions and who always offer great insights into what works in the classroom. Finally, thanks to Gordon at Kall Kwik for his design work.

Table of Contents

Introduction

Welcome to 50 Quick Ways to Use Scaffolding and Modelling. This book takes two of the most important concepts in effective, differentiated teaching and presents a whole host of practical strategies you can use to make them a central feature of your teaching.

Entries 1 – 30 focus on scaffolding, while entries 31 – 50 look at modelling. You can use the ideas across the curriculum and with a range of different age groups. I have tried to give as much illustration and exemplification as possible, so as to show what the strategies, activities and techniques look like when put into practice.

It is worth briefly explaining some of the differences between scaffolding and modelling, as well as how they connect. Scaffolding is all the things you do to help students get to grips with a task, activity or idea. It is the support you provide which scaffolds the learning; that extra bit of help students need to make progress and successfully engage with what you have planned. With that said, scaffolding should not mean the teacher doing the work for the student – and there is a great scaffolding rule of thumb connected to this in Entry One.

Modelling is where we model something for students – be that thinking, how to complete an activity, how to answer a particular question type and so on. In one sense then, modelling is a type of scaffolding. However, it is worth considering separately because of the breadth of potential strategies and teacher actions it covers. And that is why I have separated the two ideas out in this book.

All that remains to be said is that I hope you enjoy what lies ahead and to remind you that nothing is set in stone. You can adapt and modify the ideas which follow to suit your teaching style and your students. Don't be afraid to engage in a bit of trial and error to find out what works for you.

The Least Amount of Help First

01 This is a really good rule of thumb to use when you're teaching. Good scaffolding – really effective scaffolding – sees you giving the least amount of help first. This means you are not making life too easy for students. You are not doing the work or the thinking for them. And you are not failing into the trap of giving too much help (even if it's with good intentions).

If you give the least amount of help first, you leave yourself with somewhere to go. You send a message to students: first have a go yourself, making use of the initial bit of support I've offered. If it's still too difficult for them, or if they still can't quite get it, then you can come back in and offer a little bit more help.

Working in this way means tailoring your scaffolding as effectively as possible. It also means, if used over an extended period of time, that you promote a sense of agency and independent learning among your students. Scaffolding, you are implicitly saying, is the help I give to ensure you can do it yourself. That's quite a powerful message when you think about it – and quite a different one from 'let me give you as much help as I can right from the off.'

So when you are thinking about scaffolding in the context of teaching and planning, remember to use 'the least amount of help first' as a rule of thumb to guide you on your way.

Working Memory

02 Working memory is the short-term memory you use to process information in the moment. It differs from long-term memory which is where we store experiences, information and so forth. Practice helps to transfer information from working memory to long-term memory.

Psychologists are widely agreed that working memory is limited to 7 pieces of information, plus or minus two, for the majority of the population. With that in mind, consider the following:

367

2458

62389

326543

1097528

82370291

628394067

The last number contains nine digits. Remembering this without using a metacognitive strategy such as chunking is difficult. We are right at the edge of our working memory.

But what relevance does this have to scaffolding? Well, when students get stuck it is often because they are butting up against the limits of their working memory. Often, they are trying to do a number of things at once (and they may not be aware of this) which leads to a cognitive overload. So some students withdraw, give up or disengage.

Scaffolding is frequently about finding ways to make life a little bit easier for students so they can focus their working memory on the task in hand, or an aspect of it, and achieve success as a result. This point underpins many of the ideas which follow.

As an example, consider when you learned to drive. Did your instructor ask you to do everything straightaway? No. They intuitively understood that this would overload your working memory. So they broke things down. You did clutch control one week, reversing the next. Eventually, the majority of this was transferred to your long-term memory through practice. Now, I imagine, it feels like second nature.

The ZPD

03 Building on the points made in the previous entries we have Lev Vygotsky's idea of the Zone of Proximal Development (ZPD). Put simply, this suggests that all individuals have a range of things they can do, know and understand at any given point in time, a range of things currently beyond their capacities, no matter how much support they are given, and a big area in between, called the zone of proximal development, where they can learn through interaction with the environment and through scaffolding – provided by others (such as the teacher) or by themselves.

In terms of teaching and learning what this means is that all students have a subtly different ZPD. Therefore, by giving the least amount of help first we can be certain that we are always giving students every chance to put the maximum amount of effort in themselves and to find ways of being successful which are as independent as possible.

When it comes to working memory there is another important link with the ZPD. If students are pushing towards the outer edge of this (where we want them to be, as this is the area of highest challenge), they are likely also to be pushing against the limits of their working memory.

As teachers, we can identify this by observing students, listening to them, posing questions and reading their work. We can then use the conceptual model of the ZPD, along with our knowledge of the biological limitations of working memory, and the maxim 'the least amount of help first' to tailor our interventions – our scaffolding – so they match our students' needs as closely as possible.

Breaking Up the Cognitive Load

04 I like to think about scaffolding in the context of working memory as breaking up the cognitive load. Imagine a student who is really struggling to get to grips with a piece of work. We can conceive of them as having too much to try to process at this point in time. The cognitive load is too high, causing their working memory to become overloaded.

The question we now ask ourselves is: What can I do to break up the cognitive load?

Some options might be:

- Break the task down into a series of sub-tasks

- Ask the student to focus on one part of the task first

- Start the task off for the student, then ask them to take over

- Engage the student in discussion, helping them to refine and edit their thoughts before trying to apply these (rather than trying to do both at the same time)

- Give the student a piece of scrap paper and tell them to use it for notes, rough work and trial and error

Notice how, in each case, the intervention both breaks up the cognitive load, ensuring the student has slightly less to do, and doesn't try to do too much for the student too soon. The emphasis is still on the student working independently and finding their own solutions, but we are doing just enough to make the path to success accessible.

In the entries which follow we'll explore some of these examples, as well as many others, in more depth. All are underpinned by the ideas and concepts raised in these first four entries.

05 Let's visit a history lesson. The following question is on the board:

'Do you agree the Great Crash was the key turning point which paved the way for the events of the 1930s and, ultimately, World War Two?'

This is a big, complex question with a host pf possible answers. In our class we have a range of abilities. Some students jump on the question immediately and start planning an answer. Some spend some time thinking about it, discussing it with a partner, and then, feeling more confident, start to develop a plan for responding.

Others look at it and feel overwhelmed.

For this third group, we might imagine that the cognitive load is too high. There's too much in the question for them to successfully analyse at this point in time. They're being pushed just beyond the edge of their ZPD.

We intervene, finding a way to give the least amount of help first. We do this by breaking the question down into three sub-questions:

- What impact did the Great Crash have on America and Europe, in the short-term and the long-term?

- Can we rank the Great Crash above other factors which influenced the events of the 1930s?

- Was there another turning point which had a bigger impact than the Great Crash?

Now students can focus their attention – their working memory – on each question in turn. This helps them to build up an answer to the original question. The technique – dividing a question into sub-questions – is applicable across the board.

Sub-Tasks

06 As with sub-questions, so too with sub-tasks. Here's an example:

In a geography lesson the teacher sets the following task:

I want you to work in pairs to create a map of our local area. You should try to make it as accurate as possible and include all the key features.

They give students a few minutes to have a think about this and to get started. As they observe the room they notice a few pairs of students who appear to be struggling. The teacher intervenes with these pairs, scaffolding the learning by breaking the task down into a series of sub-tasks for them. These are as follows:

- Decide how much of our local area you will include in your map.

- Make a list of what you think are the most important places in our local area.

- Try some rough sketches to help you decide how big your map should be, where the different important places should go and how much space you will need to leave between them.

The principle is exactly the same as with sub-questions. We scaffold the learning by allowing students to focus their full attention on one thing at a time, avoiding cognitive overload and ensuring they can build up a successful end product, bit-by-bit.

In the spirit of giving the least amount of help first, the teacher could also have used the following strategies:

- Ask the students how the task could be divided up into three separate sub-tasks.

- Give the students two sub-tasks, both slightly more complex than the three outlined above.

- Discuss the students' ideas with them and then ask them to identify 2/3 sub-tasks based on their thinking.

Concrete Points of Reference

07 Concrete points of reference give students a way in. They provide something on which students can hang their ideas, or to which they can connect more abstract or more complex thinking. Here are some examples:

- Pose students a question and then reveal a continuum running from 'I totally agree' to 'I totally disagree'. Ask students to decide where they would place themselves on the continuum and why.

- Pose students a question and then reveal three possible answers. Ask them which of the answers most closely matches their own thoughts and why.

- Set students a task and then provide them with an example of how the task could be started. Ask them to look at this, discuss it with a partner, and then decide how they are going to begin.

- Explain a new concept to students and then re-explain it using an everyday example. For example, you might explain the concept of evaporation and then use the example of a puddle slowly evaporating through the course of a warm day.

In each of these examples we have something concrete (the continuum, the 3 possible answers, the examples) which gives students access to more complex thinking. The concrete element is like a bridge, helping students get closer to the more developed ideas. All these examples can be used across the board. You can also take the premise and apply it to create your own concrete points of reference.

Word Banks, Sentence Starters and Model Sentences

08 These help to break up the cognitive load for students, and they do so in similar ways. If students are struggling to write as fluently as they would like, you can deploy word banks, sentence starters or model sentences as a way to free up their working memory, allowing them to concentrate their efforts purely on the task of writing.

Here are some examples of what it looks like in practice:

During an English lesson, the teacher wants students to write a newspaper-style report on a recent school event. Some students are clearly struggling with this so the teacher provides a word bank – a list of perhaps ten or twelve keywords relevant to the task. These students now do not have to use as much of their effort to recall keywords and decide if they are appropriate or not. The word bank does this for them, meaning they can focus all their attention on the act of writing.

During a Science lesson, students are writing up reports of an experiment they recently conducted. The teacher sees that some students are struggling to get started and that some are OK getting started but then running into difficulties when they move from one section of the report to another. To assuage these difficulties, the teacher provides sentence starters and/or model sentences relevant to the start of each section. This gives students a scaffold from which they can work, helping them with a structural aspect of the work, so they can focus on getting the content right.

Writing Frameworks

09 Frameworks go a step further than word banks, sentence starters and model sentences. They provide students with an overarching structure into which they can place their thoughts. Because of this, they are slightly more intrusive – a touch more help is being given. However, this is often necessary. Particularly when students are writing in a certain way for the first time.

Here are some examples of writing frameworks:

- An essay framework detailing what type of information should be included at different points and how the argument should flow.

- A story template advising students on how to develop their plots, where to bring in new characters or locations and how to build up to an exciting ending.

- A report framework indicating what information needs to be included, where it needs to go and how it needs to be presented.

- A sonnet template indicating how many syllables there should be on each line, which lines should rhyme and where the stresses should lie.

- An exam question framework showing students what they need to include in each part of their answer to cover all areas of the mark-scheme.

In each example the teacher provides a framework which does some of the work for the student – namely, take care of the structure. They can then focus on practising to apply that structure and, in so doing, selecting appropriate content.

As noted, frameworks provide slightly more support than some of the ideas evinced so far. Avoid students becoming dependent by telling them that you will eventually withdraw the frameworks – and that students should have internalised them by that point.

Cues and Prompts

10 When it comes to giving the least amount of help first, cues and prompts are often the way to go. They involve the teacher intimating to students rather than telling them. The onus is on the student to use the cue or the prompt to work out what they need to do – or to remind themselves of what they already know.

A cue is a signal which indicates to students they should do something. A prompt is a stimulus which sends their thinking in a particular direction.

Here are some examples of cues, each of which subtly scaffolds the student's learning:

- A visual reminder such as a picture of a pencil (indicating that this is a writing task).

- A keyword or phrase such as '3 Before Me' (as in, try three methods of answering your question before coming to me for help).

- A reminder of something already practised, such as 'Eyes on the ball' in a PE lesson.

And here are some examples of prompts:

- 'Remind me what you need to do next' – prompting the student to focus their attention on the task and their next steps.

- 'How did we do it last lesson, can you remember?' – Prompting the student to transfer their previous experience to the current task.

- 'What comes next, is it a roll or a jump?' – A more explicit prompt in which we give students a couple of options from which to select.

Offering Choices or Options

11 You can scaffold a task for a group of students by including a set of options or choices from which they must select. The scaffolding here is in part self-directed, based on the decisions students make. It is also partly driven by the teacher, based on the set of options or choices they provide. Here is an example of what an activity of this type might look like:

Task: Create a campaign around a local issue. Choose two of the following options as the basis of your campaign:

1) Write a speech you could give to the local council convincing them that your issue needs funding and attention.

2) Produce a YouTube video you could use to inform people about your issue – and which encourages them to take action on it.

3) Create a set of posters which could go up around school, in the local area and on public transport and which draw people's attention to your issue.

4) Develop a plan outlining what your issue is, why it is a problem, what could be done about it and how doing this will effect change.

5) Design a viral marketing campaign you could use to raise awareness about your issue and to secure signatures from people who want something done about it.

Here we see the teacher providing a range of options from which students can select. Scaffolding is inherent to the activity as the options represent varying levels of difficulty, meaning different students are likely to make different choices based on where they feel they are currently at.

Clues

12 Offering students clues means giving a little bit of support but then letting them use their own thinking to get to where they want to be. This is an example of the teacher giving minimal help because clues, by their nature, still need to be unravelled, interpreted or analysed by the student.

If, after putting in some effort, the student cannot move themselves on through using the clue, then the teacher can confidently decide to step back in and give further support, safe in the knowledge that the clue didn't offer quite enough and thus more help should be given.

Here are some examples of clues:

- 'Causality might have something to do with it...'

- 'I'm thinking about Little Red Riding Hood...'

- 'Maybe there's more than one way to find the answer...'

- 'Do words always mean the same thing?'

- 'Page 38 might be worth examining...'

In each case there is ambiguity, uncertainty or a lack of clarity. This is the nature of clues. Some are easier to unravel than others (compare the fifth and the second, for example). And this throws up an additional point. When using clues, you can vary the difficulty depending on which students you are working with. To some you might give fairly straightforward clues. To others, you might give clues which are more cryptic.

Caveats in Activities

13 Introducing caveats means circumscribing the range of possible actions open to students. In so doing, you direct their efforts more precisely than would otherwise be the case. In terms of scaffolding, what we are doing here is limiting the range of potential options so students have greater certainty about what they need to do.

We do a little bit of the work for them, essentially, by saying that this, this and this needs to happen. They can then focus on making these things happen, without having to think about whether or not what they are doing is what they ought to be doing. Here is an example:

Task:

Work with a partner to practice your long passing.

Caveats:

i) Focus on using your instep. Avoid hitting the ball with other parts of your foot.

ii) When receiving the ball, concentrate on killing the pace.

The caveats provide students with information they can use to ensure the practice in which they engage is as accurate and targeted as possible. For some students in the class the caveats will be irrelevant – because they are doing them already. But for other, currently less able, students, the caveats provide valuable guidance. Guidance that the students would struggle to give themselves.

You can use caveats within any activity. They can be shared at the start of a task or, you can let the task start, observe how students are engaging with it, and then bring some in if necessary.

Success Criteria

14 We are all familiar with success criteria. They are the criteria against which work or learning is judged. The closer the work or learning is to the criteria, the better. If it surpasses the criteria, fantastic.

When sharing success criteria with students, demonstrate how these can be used to target effort, check learning and assess what to do next. Modelling this gives students a good insight into how they can take control of the success criteria and use them to direct their own efforts.

For example, we might share a set of three success criteria with students at the beginning of an extended activity. As we do, we would talk students through what the success criteria mean and give some examples of how they can be used to make decisions, assess work and judge whether or not we are heading along the right lines.

We are showing students how they can use success criteria to scaffold their own learning. The criteria make clear what is been worked towards. Therefore, students can use them as a supporting tool; something to help them keep their work on track.

If using this technique, be sure to leave the success criteria on display throughout. Otherwise, students' use of them may decline as time progresses.

Crib Sheets

15 A crib sheet contains information relevant to the task in hand. It is a collection of useful knowledge, stored on a sheet so that the user does not have to keep recalling and recollecting. Instead, they can let the crib sheet do the remembering for them, meaning they can focus on applying the information.

Here are some classic examples of crib sheets:

- In a physics lesson, students have a crib sheet containing commonly used formulae.

- In a chemistry lesson, students have a crib sheet reminding them of the common mistakes made when trying to balance chemical equations.

- In a maths lesson, students have a crib sheet reminding them of the rules of multiplying and dividing fractions.

And here are some more unusual examples of crib sheets:

- In a PE lesson, students have a crib sheet reminding them of different ways a football team can respond to tactical changes made by the opposition.

- In a literacy lesson, students have a crib sheet containing pictures which represent different features of a poem.

- In a graphic design lesson, students have a crib sheet in the form of a colour wheel.

In all these examples, the crib sheet scaffolds the learning. It does a little bit of the work for the student – but no more. It is still up to them to use the information contained in the crib sheet. But, by storing the information in this way, we have freed up the student's working memory. They can then focus this on the processes of application.

Worked Examples

16 If a student is struggling to complete a task we might conclude that they are presently unable to do what is needed to be successful. Or, it might be that they have an idea but, due to lack of practice, do not possess the confidence or past experience to put their idea into action.

In either case, worked examples are a way we can scaffold learning, helping students overcome these difficulties.

A worked example presents students with a model (and there is overlap here with modelling) of how to go about the current task. This gives them a starting point for producing their own work. If the student was previously unable to engage successfully with the activity, now they have a model which demonstrates an appropriate method they might employ. If they lacked confidence and/or experience, now they possess confirmatory information regarding what works and how to go about doing it.

You can provide worked examples for the whole class, for individuals and for groups. You can 'show' your working to students verbally or in writing. In the first case, we talk students through what we have done. In the second case, we write notes or provide annotations to achieve the same end.

A final point to consider is the depth of explanation you include in your worked examples. Always consider the student or students in front of you. Too deep an explanation might be overwhelming for some. This can then lead to a general rejection of the worked example.

I Start, You Finish

17 And it goes a little something like this…

Teacher: How are you finding the task, Saida?

Student: It's too hard, sir. I don't know what to do.

Teacher: OK, how about I start things off, and then you finish? Now, the first thing I would do is analyse the question, so let's have a look at it. Hmmm…The keywords are describe and explain, so that would make me think I should do one first, then the other. And then, just to get me started, I might do a quick spider diagram of all the things I know about internal combustion. How does that sound?

Student: So I should start by describing internal combustion and then explain how it works? And do a spider diagram first, to get my thoughts down on paper?

Teacher: Sounds good to me! Give me a shout when you're half way through and we'll have another chat.

In this, admittedly idealised, example, the teacher gives less help than they could. They show the student how to start their work off, essentially illustrating the thought process they would apply if faced with such a question. The student is then expected to finish things off – to take the start the teacher has provided and make it their own.

You can apply the principle in a wide variety of settings. The level of detail required to start things off will vary depending on the student in question. In some cases, you might need to return earlier than half-way through to check that the student has successfully interpreted your support.

Probing Questions

18 Here are some examples of probing questions:

- What do you mean by that?

- Can you give me any evidence for that?

- What examples support what you've just said?

- You said that change is inevitable, does that apply to the past as well as the present?

- Can you take a step back and tell me where your opinion comes from?

- If that's your answer, how did you arrive at it?

- Can you talk me through your thinking?

- Can you show me how you worked it out?

- If you had to convince me that what you've said is right, how would you do it?

- But why might someone give a different answer?

These types of question push, stretch and challenge student thinking. The aim is to develop student understanding so that it becomes more nuanced. Question 5, for example, is designed to make the student think about the reasons, knowledge and understanding on which their opinion rests. This results in different thinking compared to if we let the student state their opinion without exploring its origins.

Probing questions scaffold learning because they let the teacher guide the student towards ways and areas of thinking which might otherwise have been ignored or overlooked. Question 10, for example, ask students to consider what they have probably not yet thought about. In terms of learning, we are gently, subtly pushing students beyond where they have reached themselves. We are scaffolding the next level of understanding.

Ignoramus Questions

19 Here are some examples of ignoramus questions:

- Can you explain that again?

- I don't understand – can you help me?

- What does that mean?

- How can I get my head around this?

- What exactly is an ecosystem?

- What do I need to know to understand that?

- Can you walk me through it from the beginning?

- Come again?

- I need you to start again from the top. Can you do that for me?

- Have I got this right?

Playing the role of ignoramus means pretending to have no clue about what students are telling you. Through questioning of this type you bounce the onus of explanation back onto students. They then have to do more work. For example, Question 5 might come after a student has given an answer in which they talk about ecosystems. Playing the ignoramus over the meaning of the word 'ecosystem' means the student has to explain this and, in so doing, offer further qualification and analytical explanation of their original answer.

Ignoramus questioning scaffolds student learning by pushing them to think more carefully about elements of their understanding which they might otherwise take for granted. It guides students through additional practice and verbal rehearsal – work in which they might otherwise not engage.

Midwife Questions

20 Here are some examples of midwife questions:

- Do you mean…?

- How can I help you to explain your ideas?

- Shall we try talking about it in a different way?

- What might make it easier to explain?

- Could we put it like this…?

- How might we start talking about the topic?

- Can you remember a good strategy you used in the past?

- What makes this particular answer interesting/useful/special?

- If we were going to explain the idea together, how might we do it?

- What examples could you use to help me understand?

Midwife questioning sees us helping students give birth to ideas. In each of the above examples the emphasis is on prompting students to think in certain ways which make it easier for them to articulate their ideas. Question 3, for example, implies that talking in a different way might help the teacher and student to develop a shared understanding.

When we use midwife questioning we give students gentle nudges in certain directions. Question 10, for example, nudges the student towards giving examples – but also thinking about examples which specifically help the teacher to understand what is being said.

It is this nudging of thinking which forms the basis of the scaffolding. Without the midwife questioning the student is unlikely to direct their thought in the ways we know will be helpful to them. By questioning in this manner we take students above and beyond what they are able – or inclined – to do themselves.

Video Demos

21 Consider this:

A Food Technology teacher wants to help their students improve how they present food they have cooked. The focus is on making their food look more appealing; closer to how it might be presented in a restaurant.

The teacher decides to record themselves dressing a plate of food, decorating a cake, and commenting on a dish they were served in a restaurant. They turn these into three short demo videos.

At the start of the lesson, instead of talking students through what they want them to do, they send them off to a computer, tablet or smartphone to watch the videos they've created. Then, they draw the class back together and explain the purpose of the lesson. In addition, they indicate that students should go back to the videos during the lesson and use them for support when presenting their own food.

So what has the teacher done here in terms of scaffolding?

Well, the videos are a way in which the teacher can capture their own expertise, and share it with students in a format that is easy to review and replay. This means students have a reference point to which they can return in order to develop and refine their own skills. For example, a student who is struggling to ice their cake neatly can go back to the video and identify the differences between their technique and the technique the teacher is using.

This system – video-based access to expertise – underpins the huge popularity of 'how to' videos now found on YouTube.

Step-By-Step Instructions

22 At first glance, it might seem that step-by-step instructions run counter to our guiding rule of thumb: give the least amount of support first.

This is true in general, but there are at least three exceptions where step-by-step instructions are an appropriate and useful form of scaffolding:

- **When introducing complex processes.** If a process is sufficiently complex then this is likely to push student thinking to the limit. Working memory may become overloaded and, therefore, it is reasonable to begin the learning with step-by-step instructions. In this situation, those instructions will be the least amount of help first; it's just that the least amount happens to be quite a lot because of the complexity of the process.

- **When working with students who find the work extremely difficult.** If a student is finding a piece of work extremely difficult then this is a sign that they are right at the edge of their ZPD and that their own attempts at scaffolding, as well as our attempts, haven't yet hit the spot. Therefore, step-by-step instructions become a reasonable option as we know that they will help the student to work through their difficulties in a way that is methodical and carefully broken down.

- **When introducing students to something completely new.** If you know that the students you teach have little prior knowledge connected to a new topic, then step-by-step instructions might be a suitable measure on which to call. This reflects the fact that students will need to assimilate a lot of information from the off, and that they will also have to find ways in which to connect this to what they do already know and understand.

Making Space For Trial and Error

23 Trial and error plays an integral part in learning. It is through trial and error that we test things out, make mistakes and elicit information we can use to change things for the better. It is also an opportunity to practice – and to engage in active practice, in which our attention is fully focussed on the task in hand, increasing the likelihood that we will secure new knowledge and understanding quickly and successfully.

Making space for trial and error means making space in which students can self-scaffold. This is because the process of trial and error helps students to unlock what works and what doesn't. Armed with this information, they can alter what they do and what they think. This sees them moving themselves further up their own ZPD, and increasing the range of what they can do unassisted.

Trial and error can be built into most activities. One simple option is to include regular opportunities for discussion and verbal rehearsal. Speech is ephemeral. Students often find it easier and safer to make mistakes in conversation than in writing or in a task proper.

You can increase the impact of trial and error by talking to students about the process and giving them question prompts to use while they are doing it. For example, you might tell students to ask themselves the following questions after each trial:

- Did it work? Why?

- How could I change things next time?

- What have I learned from this effort?

That's Wrong...

24 There's nothing wrong with saying something's wrong. If a student hasn't got an answer right, they need to know. But if 'that's wrong' is the end of the discussion, well that's bad news. But if 'that's wrong' is the start of the discussion, well that's great. Here are four examples:

Teacher A: 'That's wrong' (walks off)

Teacher B: 'That's wrong. Why do you think it might be wrong? Have a look and tell me what you think.'

Teacher C: 'Interesting...that's wrong. I wonder how you got to that answer. Let's have a chat about it and see what happened with your thinking.'

Teacher D: 'That's wrong. Have a chat with your partner and see if you can work out why. I'll come back in a minute and we'll have a chat about it.'

The four teachers all tell the student in question that they've got an answer wrong. B, C and D use this as an opportunity to support the learning. Whereas A leaves the student hanging. Now, in some case, and with some students, that might be OK. These students might be sufficiently self-motivated and self-aware to take that as a prompt to go back and root out the cause of their being wrong.

But, for many students, the scaffolding provided by B, C and D is a better option. In each case, the teacher offers a little bit of help to direct the student into thinking critically about their wrong answer. They make it into the start of a discussion. One in which they might end up having to give more help, or not, depending on how the discussion goes.

Verbal Rehearsal

25 I mentioned verbal rehearsal in passing a couple of entries ago, when we were thinking about trial and error. The technique is a useful scaffolding tool; one you can apply in many settings.

Verbal rehearsal is when students have the chance to practice verbalising their ideas. They might do this once, twice or a number of times. The type of activity you use and the context of the lesson will determine this.

When we verbalise our thoughts we have a chance to practice, refine and edit them. Through this process we grow more confident in understanding what we think, and tend to increase the quality and coherence of our thinking. Here are three examples of teachers using verbal rehearsal to scaffold student learning in lessons:

- A science teacher invites their students to talk through how they will carry out an experiment before doing it. They have three opportunities to do this in quick succession.

- An economics teacher asks their students to talk through the arguments for and against nationalised industries, giving pairs ninety seconds in which to do this, prior to planning an essay on the topic.

- A primary school teacher challenges their students to talk though how they will design a piece of art work they are making for Mother's Day.

In each case, the verbal rehearsal scaffolds learning by letting students refine, edit and test their ideas before putting them into practice.

Scrap Paper

26 Here's a sum for you to try:

527 x 328

How would you approach it?

My strategy would be take a piece of scrap paper, write the sum down, break it into segments (500 x 328; 20 x 328; 7 x 328), record the result of each of these and then total them up for the overall answer.

There are other methods, of course. But this one illustrates a central fact about scrap paper: it is one of the easiest ways in which to expand the capacity of working memory. In the example, I do not have to hold all the information in my head. I know that, for me, this won't be possible. Instead, I use the scrap paper to store first the three separate sums, then the three separate answers. I use my working memory to solve the sums and to then total the answers.

This leads us to the conclusion that encouraging students to use scrap paper on a regular basis means giving them a tool through which they can self-scaffold. You might like to think of it as metacognitive strategy.

While simple, students often overlook it. They either forget to use it or think there is something wrong in making recourse to the method. Disabusing them of this idea is important. Showing them how to use scrap paper, encouraging its use, and even providing rough books are all worthy routes to go down.

Note Down Your Thoughts

27 Noting down thoughts works in a similar way to using scrap paper. Let us imagine we have just posed a question to the class. Immediately on finishing we say 'Think about your answer and then, when you're ready, note down your thoughts.'

This supplement to the question directs students to externalise their thinking and to fix it in time and space through the act of writing. Having done this, they then have a permanent record of their initial thoughts. This frees up working memory. They no longer have to hold onto these thoughts because they are written down.

It also gives students a chance to look at their thoughts, read them through and question whether what they have written is right, whether it accurately represents what they think and whether it could be improved, developed or added to.

So the simple act of noting down thoughts actually serves to scaffold the process of thinking quite considerably. Getting into the routine of appending your questions with 'note down your thoughts' means getting into the routine of helping students to scaffold their thinking. By drawing attention to what is happening you also make students consciously aware of the process. This helps them to understand it, internalise it and, over time, use it without needing to be told.

Thinking Time

28 Another way to scaffold student thinking when posing questions is through the provision of thinking time. Consider the difference between these two examples:

Teacher A: 'What made the story exciting? John, what do you think?'

Teacher B: 'What made the story exciting? Thirty seconds silent thinking.' (30 seconds elapse) 'John, what do you think?'

Teacher B scaffolds student learning by providing space in which to think. This thinking time allows John to divide his attention between thinking about the question (during the thirty seconds) and thinking about how to articulate his thoughts to the teacher and the class.

Some students will always be able to give an immediate answer. But even with these learners, the scaffolding adds something. During the thinking time we can expect them to go beyond the first answer which came into their heads – developing their thinking as a result.

You may have heard thinking time referred to as wait time. Both phrases mean the same thing. Both refer to the teacher slowing down and giving students space in which to process what has been said and identify what they think about it.

Training yourself to give thinking time after posing a question means training yourself to scaffold student learning every time a question is posed.

Which answer do you like most?

29 Even after using the techniques listed in the last four entries – verbal rehearsal, noting down thoughts, scrap paper and wait time – some students may still struggle to answer the questions you pose.

This can be for all manner of reasons: lack of confidence, uncertainty, perceived ambiguity, genuine ambiguity, perceived costs of answering incorrectly, a hazard view of mistakes, lack of knowledge and understanding.

One way to help such students is to scaffold your questioning rather more extensively. You can do this by posing a question and then presenting a selection of answers (either verbally or visually) before asking the student which answer they like the most and why.

Here, we are working on the assumption that the student's ZPD is, at present, somewhat behind their peers. To help push it on we provide answers instead of asking students to do this. Two benefits accrue. First, the student gets to see what possible answers can look like or hear what they can sound like. Second, they are given an accessible way in. No longer do they have to develop an answer themselves. Instead, they can choose an existing answer and comment on this (a much simpler process).

If students respond well to this scaffolding we can quickly push them on and challenge their thinking by asking them to justify their choice of answer, to contrast their choice with a different option, or to suggest another possible answer which has been overlooked.

Simplification

30 If a student is struggling to access a piece of work, we might decide to change the nature of that work. This is as an alternative to providing a tool or support which helps students to access the work without changing its level.

One of the best ways to make work more accessible is through simplification. This is scaffolding because it involves the teacher observing how the learner is interacting with a task and then intervening to change the level of difficulty based on what they see. Here are five examples:

- In a business studies lesson the teacher simplifies a set of company accounts. The student is now able to apply their currently limited knowledge of how to read accounts.

- In a maths lesson the teacher gives a small group of students a set of equations to solve containing only one unknown quantity, while the rest of the class work on equations with two or three unknown quantities.

- In a philosophy lesson the teacher uses common rather than technical language to describe key ethical systems.

- In a history lesson the teacher asks a student to compare three sources instead of five. Or, they ask a student to contrast one key feature of five sources, rather than a range of features.

- In a science lesson, the teacher removes a variable from an experiment so a group of students can concentrate on understanding the effects of a single variable first, before looking at combined effects.

What is modelling?

31 At this point we move from scaffolding to modelling, though it goes without saying that the two are closely connected – and that modelling can often be a form of scaffolding, depending on how, when and why it is used. To avoid getting bogged down, let us define modelling thus: a process by which the teacher shows students how to do something; the teacher provides a model that students can imitate, adapt or borrow from.

Seen in this light, modelling encompasses a great many actions the teacher can take – when they are teaching, as part of their planning and as part of their assessment processes.

One of the hallmarks of highly effective teaching is regular teacher modelling, including the modelling of thinking. This was highlighted in a 2014 report by The Sutton Trust: 'What makes great teaching?'

In that report, a number of teacher assessment systems from around the world were analysed. The aim was, broadly, to pick out similarities and see if there were certain common themes which could be identified as indicative of great teaching, regardless of context.

While that goal proved somewhat elusive, teacher modelling and the modelling of thinking was consistently identified, across the different systems, as a mainstay of great teaching. With that in mind, let us look at a variety of ways you can use it in the classroom.

Demonstrating Techniques

32 A technique is a skill or process. Demonstrating techniques means providing students with a model of how to execute a specific skill or process. There are many ways in which this can be done. Examples include:

- The teacher standing at the front of the class and showing all students

- The teacher demonstrating in front of small groups or individual students

- The teacher recording themselves executing the technique (possibly with narration as well)

The approach gains in efficacy when the demonstration is accompanied by verbal communication of expertise. For example, a Design and Technology (DT) teacher might be demonstrating to their whole class how to solder. If they show the technique and say nothing while doing this, then the students are not gaining access to the expert understanding stored inside the teacher's head. They are only gaining access to the visual model provided through the teacher's physical demonstration of the technique.

Supplementing your demonstration with narration and commentary means drawing students' attention to things you know about the technique but which might not be immediately obvious. For example, our DT teacher might explain what happens if too much or too little solder is used and how they work out the right amount to apply.

When commenting on your demonstration of technique, try to talk about potential mistakes and errors as much as the correct way of doing things. This gives students a heads up about what could go wrong, why it might happen and what can be learned from it.

Modelling a Contrast

33 Here we show students how two things differ. The aim is to develop their understanding by highlighting the general nature of the contrast and the specific elements which make it up. Here is an example to demonstrate:

In an English lesson focussing on speech writing the teacher begins by giving two different speeches to the class. The first speech focuses exclusively on logos – appeals to logic and reason. The second speech focuses exclusively on pathos – appeals to emotions and feelings.

During the two speeches, the teacher pauses at opportune moments so they can talk students through what is happening, why it is happening and what effect the teacher intends this to have on the audience. At the end of the two speeches they lead the class in a discussion of the differences between the two approaches. This serves as a powerful way through which to draw out the strengths and weaknesses of using logos and pathos as part of your attempts to sway an audience.

The example illustrates the way in which modelling a contrast can make abstract differences between different ideas or processes quickly come to life. This is because the information is embodied in what the teacher does. Instead of just talking about the differences students are seeing them (or hearing them) and then talking about what they've seen.

Subject-Specific Models

34 Many modelling techniques are applicable across the board. You can use them with different age groups and in different areas of the curriculum. Take the last entry – modelling a contrast. We could use it to model a contrast in the texture of materials for very young children and to model a contrast in the interpretation of Macbeth by different directors for young adults.

Subject-specific models are those models which don't necessarily transfer. They are unique to a particular subject, reflecting the nature of that subject – both its content and the way in which it is taught. Here are some examples:

- Modelling the structure of an atom in physics.

- Modelling how to disguise a slower ball when bowling in cricket.

- A model showing how to identify failing companies in business studies.

- A model showing how to dissect a frog in biology.

- Modelling how to test code in computing.

In each of these cases we have a process which is specific to the subject and which, in a number of cases, is fairly technical. While some of the underlying premises can be transferred (for example, the use of representative objects or diagrams in the first example), the model as a whole cannot.

This emphasises that what you teach can play in role in determining the kind of modelling you do. It also suggests that identifying and developing subject-specific models as part of your planning can be highly effective.

Critiquing Models

35 If we model something for our students, or present them with a model which someone else has developed, should we expect them to accept it uncritically?

I pose the question because I do not believe the answer is as simple as it might seem. On the one hand we might say yes. After all, is not the point of us modelling something that students take on board what we have shown them, either to imitate or adapt?

On the other hand, do we want students to blindly accept the models we show them; to unquestioningly take on board the modelling we do?

The tension here is between making best use of modelling and helping students to think critically about the ideas, skills and processes we present to them.

Paying heed to this means deciding whether, on occasion, it is worth helping students critique the models to which you introduce them. For example, a history teacher might present students with a model for analysing sources. After this has been employed for a few lessons, they may then start to problematize it, asking students whether it really is as good as it seems.

One of the most effective points at which to encourage criticism of models is during transition phases. For example, if a student is moving from GCSE to A Level study, we might encourage them, in the first few lessons of A Level, to critique the models they used at GCSE. This promotes a critical mindset and highlights the fact that they will have to learn new approaches and cannot expect to rely on what they have previously used.

Providing the Bare Bones

36 When modelling something for your students you do not always have to give them the full picture. In fact, giving them the bare bones is often a good way to help them begin a task. They can then develop further ideas and make the activity their own:

In a geography lesson the teacher models how to build up an accurate map from a set of observations. However, they do this in a fairly broad brush manner, focussing on generalities and major points without going into much detail. They make their students aware of this, explaining what is happening. This avoids confusion and any sense on the part of the students that they have been short-changed.

Next, the teacher asks students to make their observations and to then use these to construct a map. A set of success criteria are displayed on the board. The level of detail needed to achieve these goes beyond what the teacher modelled.

In this example we see the benefit of a 'bare bones' modelling technique. The teacher has given students enough to get started, but there is still scope for them to push themselves, develop their own ideas and engage in some trial and error in an attempt to get things right.

Record Yourself

37 A fun alternative to modelling in front of students is to record yourself in advance and then play the video during the lesson. Here are some examples of how it can work:

- A primary school teacher records themselves using a number chart to solve number problems.

- An art teacher records themselves throwing a bowl on a potter's wheel.

- A maths teacher records themselves using trial and error to find the value of X.

- A religious studies teacher records themselves reading a religious text for meaning.

- A psychology teacher records themselves evaluating a psychological study.

As mentioned elsewhere, videos of this type benefit from narration (and this pretty much has to be the case in example number four). They are an innovative and interesting way to model ideas and processes. It is also possible for students to watch them multiple times. This can help them as they practice and also allows for detailed scrutiny.

Finally, you might like to consider building up a bank of videos you can use year after year. Identify the key areas where modelling is going to be particularly useful and start making relevant short films. An added benefit is that you can then set students the task of watching some or all of these at the start of the year or at the beginning of individual topics.

Exemplar Work Bank

38 Exemplar work offers students a model of how to complete a task, activity or challenge. An exemplar work bank is a selection of work, collated by the teacher, to which students can turn when they want help or guidance. The work can be annotated (giving an insight into the thinking which underpins the finished product) or it can be left as it is, with students having to work out why it is good or what allowed the creator to be successful.

Here are some examples of exemplar work banks, showing how they can differ from subject to subject:

- In PE, a collection of videos showing athletes in a variety of disciplines performing skills with a high level of technical accuracy.

- In art, a collection of paintings produced by a range of students, all of which demonstrate effective use of specific techniques.

- In literacy, a selection of stories written by children in years gone by, all of which show different qualities of skilled story-writing.

- In philosophy for children, a selection of discussion summaries in which the general level of conversation was consistently critical, creative and cooperative.

Unpicking Model Answers

39 Model answers come via one of three routes: created by the teacher, provided by an exam board, or created by students. Unpicking model answers sees you and your students chipping away at what has been presented in an effort to get underneath the surface and work out why this is a model answer. What is it about it that makes it good? Why was the creator able to construct it – what did they need to know and what did they need to be able to do?

The process of unpicking a model answer is a process of helping students understand what went into its creation. In this sense, it is something of a backwards journey. We are starting with the end – the finished article – and winding our way slowly backwards so we can understand the path which led to the final product.

When first using this technique you will need to direct proceedings to a large extent. The first few attempts are as much about students learning how to unpick model answers as they are about students taking on board the insights elicited.

A good approach is to present students with a set of questions you, as an expert, would ask of any model answer you encountered. For example:

- Why is this a model answer?

- What does this answer show, do or demonstrate?

- How does it meet the success criteria or match up with the mark-scheme?

- What steps did the creator take to produce it?

- What ideas, strategies and techniques can I borrow from it?

Modelling Questioning

40 We ask hundreds of questions every day. Questioning is the main way through which teachers interact with students. This is unusual. In most social situations questions don't have such a significant role. It reflects the nature of the teacher-student relationship; the rules of the teacher-student game.

Modelling questioning means attending to the type of questions you are asking and drawing students' attention to these questions – both their nature and the way in which you go about constructing them.

Doing this brings about a considerable benefit. It helps students understand how they can ask better questions themselves. These questions will go in one of three directions – to the teacher, to a peer, or to themselves (such as when we question ourselves in our own mind while attempting a task or trying to work out a tricky problem).

In each case, the quality of the student's question influences the response they receive. Better questions tend to receive better responses (though this can't be guaranteed).

If you want to pursue this idea further, a nice next step is to create questioning crib sheets. For example, think back to entries 18, 19 and 20, where we exemplified three specific questioning styles. You could create a crib sheet for students modelling these three styles, with examples, relevant question stems and suggestions of when and where to use them.

Modelling Thinking

41 Modelling thinking is vitally important because it give students direct access to your expertise as a thinker. They can then use this to change how they think – to develop, refine and adapt their thinking. This is why, for me, the modelling of thinking is very close to feedback in terms of what is happening in the interaction between teacher and students. Just as with the provision of feedback, the aim is to help students change what they do by making use of the information presented by the teacher.

There are many ways to model thinking, some of which we will explore in the following entries. However, one often overlooked point is the benefit which can accrue from drawing students' attention to what you are doing. This means you both model your thinking *and* make students aware of what you are doing.

Working in this way promotes metacognition and avoids the risk that your modelling is simply seen as another part of the wider lesson. While it is part of the wider whole it is also distinct because it is concerned with the thinking underpinning the lesson. Therefore it is both of the lesson and outside of it.

Another point to add is that you can change the complexity of your modelling depending on the students you are working with. For example, you might model your thinking in a high level of detail for some learners, but in a simple, more general way for others.

Metacognitive Past Papers

42 Here's an unusual and highly effective technique for sharing your expert thinking with students:

Take a past exam paper. Work through the paper, annotating each page. Ensure you cover every question. Do not annotate the paper with any of the answers. Instead, annotate the paper with your expert thinking. If you were sitting down to take the exam, what would you be thinking at each point? What clues and prompts would you look for? What questions would you ask yourself to keep on track?

This sees you creating a metacognitive past paper. One containing an extensive model of your thinking. Having finished, photocopy it and hand out copies to all the students in your class. Then, take a lesson to go through the paper with them. As you do, draw attention to different aspects of what you've written and facilitate discussion around the various annotations.

This technique is of particular relevance to exam classes. But you can extend it to other groups of students by creating annotated exemplars of common questions or activity types. For example, a primary school teacher might create an annotated exemplar of how to think about a story-writing task.

This provides students with a model of how to think about such tasks – which they can return to again and again, until it is internalised and becomes a part of their own minds.

Alternative Methods

43 Many of the things we ask students to do at school can be completed in a variety of different ways. For example, there are different methods of multiplication, none of which are necessarily pre-eminent.

Modelling alternative methods means showing students that there is more than one way to think about a problem or issue. This is worth doing for a couple of reasons. First, some students might find some methods easier than others – or they might just prefer one particular method without really being able to say why. Second, it is good for students to know that thought does not come pre-packaged and fully circumscribed. The implication of this is that how they think is open to change, that it can go in different directions, and that thinking in a number of different ways is no bad thing.

When modelling alternative methods you should think carefully about laying your groundwork. For example, if you have spent three lessons getting students to practice a specific method for analysing data and then, in the fourth lesson, you announce that there are a number of other ways to do it, this might cause some confusion, even some pained glances from the back of the room.

Here are three brief examples of teachers modelling alternative methods in different subject areas:

- In an art lesson, the teacher talks through three different approaches to thinking about perspective.

- In a numeracy lesson, the teacher models how to think about division in two different ways.

- In a geography lesson, the teacher models three different ways to think about maps.

Talking Through Your Thinking

44 Perhaps the most common way teachers model thinking for their students is by narrating their thinking as it happens. Here are some examples:

- A maths teacher is demonstrating how to factorise quadratic equations. They walk the class through a series of examples on the board. Each time, they talk students through their thinking as they are completing the task.

- A primary school teacher is teaching students about the structure of volcanoes. As they do, they talk though their own thinking on the topic, helping students to see connections with other areas of geography and also showing them some useful techniques for remembering key ideas.

- An economics teacher brings in a recent speech made by the Governor of the Bank of England. They give copies to students and then talk through their thinking about the speech. In the process they show students how to analyse a speech of this type and how to read between the lines of what is being said.

- A PE teacher is demonstrating how to take an attacking free kick in football. They walk students through the process of placing the ball, assessing the possible options, running up and then striking the ball correctly. At each stage they narrate their own thinking, giving students access to this expertise.

- A religious studies teacher brings in a copy of a religious text. They give photocopies to students in the class and then precede to talk through how they would analyse this text and what evidence can be used to draw out the key themes.

This technique – narrating your own thinking – can be applied in almost any setting at almost any time. It's a great way to give all students access to your expertise.

Modelling Trial and Error

45 Trial and error – or trial and improvement as some teachers like to call it – is one the key ways in which we learn. It is through trial and error that we make sense of new experiences, testing the boundaries of what is possible and responding to the information we receive.

Modelling trial and error means two things. First, you show students that this process – including the failure and mistake-making it inevitably involves – is a good thing. Something to be used, rather than avoided. Second, you show students how to use trial and error most effectively. For example, you model the process of examining why a trial went wrong, working out how to use this information to inform the next trial, and persisting even if getting to your desired end result takes a while.

So there are two elements at play here: the general modelling of trial and error as a technique and the specific modelling of the thinking which constitutes effective use of trial and error.

Here are a couple of examples to illustrate these points:

- In a sociology lesson, the teacher models the process of writing and rewriting an answer for an exam-style question. As they do, they explain how to analyse each attempt, compare it to the question and draw conclusions which can inform the next effort.

- In a drama lesson, the teacher models the process of developing a character. During this, they show students techniques they can use to assess successive efforts, and how to use the results to make improvements.

Modelling Targeted Effort

46 There are two types of effort in the classroom: useful and useless. The latter often masquerades as the former, but it will always give itself away by the results to which it leads. Sometimes, students don't realise that the effort they're putting in is useless. They find themselves running on the spot while believing that they are running towards a finish line.

Modelling targeted effort means showing students the difference between effort which has no direction and effort driven by a clear goal or purpose. Here are some examples:

- In a classics lesson the teacher models targeted effort by showing students how to identify themes, prompts and clues during the process of translation. They contrast this to students trying to translate a piece of text without recourse to any of these elements. In so doing, they point to the different results which are likely to follow.

- In a graphic design lesson the teacher shows students how to interpret a design brief using a range of existing stylistic themes, motifs and movements. They contrast this with unthinking repetition, drawing attention to the act of interpretation as the point at which targeted effort really takes place.

- In an English lesson the teacher models how to read actively, contrasting this to the process of passive reading. They demonstrate how the former involves targeted effort and, as a result, a much more meaningful, and interesting, engagement with the text than the latter.

Modelling Mistake-Making

47 We touched on mistake-making two entries ago, when we looked at trial and error. Here we can examine it in more depth.

If students are reluctant to make mistakes then they may well avoid challenges and give up in the face of obstacles. This is because both of these situations involve an increased likelihood that you will get things wrong – that you will make a mistake.

As teachers, we know that mistake-making is a good thing. It provides opportunities to learn, elicits useful information and is an inevitable part of the process of practice and development.

Modelling mistake-making helps students overcome negative perceptions of failure. It lessens the sense of risk they might attach to it and gives them a method they can employ when they make their own mistakes. Here are some things to think about when you use this technique:

- Draw students' attention to the separation of emotional reactions from analytical engagement with the results of mistake-making. Explain that it's OK to have an emotional reaction, but that we can acknowledge this and then put it to one side.

- Make a distinction between good mistakes (from which we can learn) and careless mistakes.

- Show how to analyse a mistake in search of information you can use to learn, make improvements and avoid the same thing happening again.

- Talk through the thinking process you adopt when interrogating the mistakes you make.

- Highlight the lack of negative consequences that mistakes tend to give rise to in most situations. Contrast reality with the false perceptions students might build up.

Modelling Responses to Being Stuck

48 When a student is stuck they have two choices open to them: to act, or not to act. If they choose the second option, this may be because they do not know how to act. They do not have the skills or experience with which to respond.

Modelling responses to being stuck is therefore about giving students the tools they need to deal successfully with difficult situations. Here are two examples of the technique in action:

- In a tennis lesson the teacher works one-on-one with a student who keeps getting beaten by their opponent's forehand. The teacher talks the student through the process of analysing what is happening. They draw their attention to different elements of the problem and highlight features of the opponent's play which, up until that point, the student was not aware of. They then compare these to what the student is doing and suggest how a change in approach could lead to different results.

- In a business studies lesson the teacher shows students how to break down scenario planning into a series of manageable steps. They emphasise that many seemingly complex tasks can be thought of as a series of separate, simpler elements. They work with the class to come up with a three-step model anybody could employ when in a similar situation.

Peer Models

49 Up until now, our focus has been on modelling by the teacher for their students. In this, our penultimate entry, we can think briefly about the benefit of peer models. These give learners a different way to think about an idea, skill or process. They provide an alternative angle – a different way into the learning.

One significant benefit of peer models is that students often talk in similar codes; codes which the teacher may struggle to access. If we can find opportunities for peers to model for each other, then we are finding opportunities for them to communicate information about the learning within the codes with which they are most familiar.

Another benefit of peer models is that students can show each other how they are doing things, with this often differing in subtle and unexpected ways from the 'ideal' model presented by the teacher. For example, I might model how to use trial and error, but a student might take this on and develop it into a way that works for them. It would then be this which they modelled for their peer.

You can use peer modelling as a supplement to your own modelling, or you can let it take centre stage.

Both options have their benefits. In the latter case, this is most useful when you have one or more students who demonstrate high levels of understanding or skill development.

Diagrams and Images

50 We conclude our journey through scaffolding and modelling with recourse to the visual. Diagrams and images are another way in which we can model ideas, processes and skills for our students. Here are some examples of how to use them:

- Illustrate ideas through diagrams. For example, we might show the idea of friction through an image of two surfaces moving past one another, with arrows and annotations describing what is happening.

- Illustrate processes through diagrams. For example, we might show the process of rural to urban migration through a diagram. This could be a general, idealised example or it could be an example of a specific geographical area, such as China.

- Demonstrate processes through contrasting images. For example, we might show students two images of defensive positioning in rugby, one which is good and one containing mistakes.

- Demonstrate ideas through images. For example, we might use images to model the idea of change for very young students.

- Illustrate skills through a sequence of diagrams. For example, we might use a series of diagrams to model the skill of hand-building with clay.

In these examples, the diagrams and images either supplement verbal or written explanation or give access to information that is hard to convey in those forms. As such, they help students better understand what they need to know to be successful.

And with that, we reach the end. I hope you've found the ideas presented in the book useful, and that they connect to your experience of teaching. Throughout my career I've found scaffolding and modelling to be two of the most powerful tools through which to support students, raise achievement and help learners to really enjoy learning. I hope you find the same, and that this book aids you in your endeavours.

A Brief Request

If you have found this book useful I would be delighted if you could leave a review on Amazon to let others know.

If you have any thoughts or comments, or if you have an idea for a new book in the series you would like me to write, please don't hesitate to get in touch at mike@mikegershon.com.

Finally, don't forget that you can download all my teaching and learning resources for **FREE** at www.mikegershon.com and www.gershongrowthmindsets.com

Made in the USA
Monee, IL
26 October 2022

16630718R00066